Ella's Children

Book One of the Tin Train Series

By Norma Jean

Denty Publications

Contents

Haunting Memories

The haunting memories,
of years gone by,
A dream remembered,
a child's cry,
I look to the past,
and wonder why,
To leave our tortured souls,
to cry.
Our healing bodies,
mind and soul,
Leave many stories,
forever untold

By Joan (Baas) McQuirt

Dedication

Dedicated to my mother, Ella Loree Lamb.

Without her love, none of this would be possible.

She always told us "Look to God and pray my child, that good people influence your life."

I thank God every day for His countless blessings, and for watching over me.

Much thanks to my brothers and sisters, for their support and help in writing this book.

Thanks to Pastor Thomas Phillips for his support and encouragement. Even when I wanted to quit he wouldn't let me.

Thanks to Elizabeth Coutellier for her editing and suggestions.

A great big thanks to my Daughter Erika, who grew up in a house with a mom who was dysfunctional. She loves me anyway.

Last of all to my husband Jeff without his love, support and rewritten drafts this book would not have happened.

Preface

I started with when I was three years old because it is my earliest recollection of my child hood of things not being normal. Things in my house hold were strange and ugly. Today I struggle with the added burden that my grandchildren are asking questions of what my childhood was like.

My grandson knows I am writing about my childhood and he has promised to finish it for me should something happen to me before it is finished. He is already writing way better than I ever did and he is only ten years old. He is already better at critiquing than I am even today. He can read a story and tell you what is missing. The first time I let him read one of my stories he told me exactly what was wrong and how to fix it. I thought that was the coolest thing.

God has blessed me in so many ways so I wanted to give back in the only way I could. He has planted these ideas in my head all my life to write down for the Next Generation. So they would never forget and go back to what was.

If you see yourself in any of these situations do your children a favor and ask God to help you stop. With Him all things are possible. We can do nothing without Him.

These are my childhood memories. This is how I remember my childhood.

8

A Child's fury

I was just four years old, when I watched as my dad dragged my mother into the bathroom by her hair. She was kicking and screaming the whole way. She was trying to put up a good fight. Dad ignored her screams of anguish. He was drunk again and oblivious to her pain.

I don't know why I chose today to do something about it. The bathroom was only three feet by four feet. It was the smallest room in the house. It was pale blue. The ceiling and baseboards were painted white. But the paint that was once a luxurious sky blue is now dingy and dirty and chipped and peeling. I never noticed these things before. It is funny how trauma can make innocence disappear. Dad's grease smears were everywhere just like the rest of the house. Little children's hand prints were everywhere. The baseboards that were once white had become a dingy gray. There wasn't enough money for food let alone for repairs on the house. The linoleum was bare and worn. You could see the black tar that was the under layer. In today's world the black would mean asbestos. From so many people sharing the same bathroom day in and day out it needed replaced.

My dad did not waste any time getting on top of her. He shoved her onto the commode. He was straddling her pushing his manhood into her. She was screaming, "don't Art it hurts! Stop! Please stop! I don't want to, it hurts." She was crying. I ran into the bathroom. I was going to protect my Mother. I didn't know I was too little. The thought never entered my mind. I was already taking care of the younger kids. I started pounding my tiny little fists on my dad's back. I wanted to try and make him stop. It didn't work. He took his arm and flung me aside like I was an unwanted flea or a gnat. I went flying across the bathroom floor. I bumped my head on the wall. It hurt. I had a big bump. I had a bloody lip. Tears were streaming down my face. My tears were mixed with the blood on my face. I didn't know if I was crying for me or for my mother. But I got up and started doing it again. I took my tiny little fist and beat my dad's back. Again he flung me aside. I did it again and again. I told my dad, "Don't you hurt my mother anymore. Can't you see you are hurting her?" I was not going to quit. I was going to keep going back to beat him until he quit. I wasn't hurting him at all though.

There was blood everywhere I looked. There was blood on the toilet seat. There was blood on the floor. There was blood on the walls mixed with the grease and fingerprints. This blood wasn't mine. I thought he was killing her. She had just given birth to twins two weeks earlier.

It was my mother who finally stopped me. I heard her say, "Art the children. Think of the children." I went back to do it again to beat my fists on him. My mother looked up at me with those sad resigned eyes that were swollen and black. She said, "Norma don't! I don't want what is happening to me to happen to you. Please go, leave the bathroom." I didn't need to be told twice. I didn't want this to happen to me either. My mother was bleeding I thought my dad had done this to her. My dad had her held down onto the toilet seat. He was raping her. Day in and day out he raped her. He seemed to be oblivious to her pain and suffering.

I didn't want him to do this to me. I didn't know if he would. I didn't know if my mother was just trying to scare me. She succeeded in scaring me enough that it made an imprint on my life forever. My Dad scared me too. I never forgot it. I never forgot my dad on top of my mother. She was bleeding. I just knew it hurt her. I was ashamed that I couldn't help. I was ashamed that I was too little to make a difference in someone's life. I was ashamed that I was too scared to continue to help my mother. I was ashamed that I had witnessed this.

My mother was a small woman. She was five feet tall and weighed a hundred pounds. She had dark brown almost black hair and brown eyes. She was mild mannered and quiet. She spoke softly. She had a quality of regal bearing that stemmed from her deep faith in God. She prayed every day that God get her through just one more day. She also prayed for God to keep her children safe. One could see the Holy Spirit deep within her soul if you just looked into her eyes. Her faith kept her going. I saw the Bible opened daily and her reading. She was trying to make her miserable life a life worth living. God gave her lots of children to nurture. She loved each and every one of us. Even if she could not show it every day she loved us. We were never far from her mind.

My dad was five feet ten and a half inches tall. He weighed over two hundred and ten pounds. It didn't matter who was watching or who was around when dad was drunk and wanted sex he took it. He reeked of alcohol. You could smell it on him. The whole house seemed to ooze of alcohol. He would spill it or slosh it around. If the wind blew just right his very pores seemed to ooze with alcohol. His eyes were always bloodshot. His nose was bulbous and red. When he was drunk, which was most of the time, he did what he wanted, when he wanted and no one could stop him. In our house he was god. There weren't any laws for protecting women and children back then. Men were a law to themselves. They were allowed to do to their families whatever they wanted, whenever they wanted, with whom they wanted. It was the same thing day in and day out Dad would come home drunk. He would grab hold of my mother's hair or grabbed her arm and practically pushed her or pulled her into the bathroom.

I hid out under the bed the rest of the day. It seemed to be the only safe place to hide. I hid there. The Omar bread box was the only other place that was safe. We used it as a dirty clothes hamper. It was big enough for kids to hide in. I used to day dream about having a safe hideout. I never found one. I used to day dream there was a secret door with a small chamber at the stairway just above the stairs. I could go and hide out there.

There were so many kids there just wasn't enough space in the tiny two bed-room house for eleven children to have a place of their own. I cried and cried. No one ever came looking for me that day either. It was like I didn't exist. No one seemed to care that I had just bombarded the bathroom. Mom and dad were in there doing whatever they were doing.

We called our mom, "mother" but we never called our dad, "father." Only God was elevated to that status. I always thought it was a sign of lack of respect. Dad didn't deserve our respect. He was our dad yes! He didn't respect anyone or anything. So we in turn learned not to respect him. That is not to say we diso-beyed him. We didn't disobey our dad. His punishments were outlandish and brutal. You got beaten with whatever he could get a hold of at the time.

I truly wanted to help my mother as little as I was. There wasn't anything I could do. It didn't make me feel any better. It made me feel more and more ashamed, that I couldn't help my mother from getting all the abuse. I was sickened and saddened but I just couldn't help her. It was humiliating to me to think that all of this was going on. That no one could stop the abuse. I felt like the shame was almost worse than the abuse. This shame was hidden. No one could see it. The shame of being so small and not having the strength to make my dad stop the abuse, the shame of knowing God didn't want us to hurt anyone yet dad was doing just that.

This scene would live in my head and be replayed over and over again. It left its mark on me. I understood what shame was. It was the beginning of a lifetime of shame. I felt my mother's pain and humiliation. I felt what my mother must have wanted for her children. She wanted us to have a better life instead of this degradation. There wasn't any turning back the clock wishing that I hadn't gone in there because I did go in there.

I was mad. I was frustrated. I wasn't big enough to stop him. I did not understand why my older brothers and sisters didn't try to stop him. I did not understand why the neighbors didn't stop him. The windows were wide open. There was no way the neighbors could not hear the screams. The screams were loud. But no one ever came. No one called the police. Everyone in the neighborhood walked past as though they heard nothing. At least pretended they heard nothing. They seemed to cross to the other side. They avoided our end of the block. They would not look us in the eye like they knew and they too were ashamed. It did not make us feel better to feel their shame as well.

I made a promise to protect all of my brothers and sisters to the best of my abilities to not let harm come to them. I would protect them and try to keep them safe.

By the time I was four there were ten children, five boys and five girls. I had two younger brothers and two younger sisters. Of this four there was a set of twins, a girl and a boy. I was my mother's right hand. I helped her out whenever and wherever she needed help. I loved helping my mother. I was always called mothers little helper. All young girls love helping their mothers. It wasn't drudgery to me. I loved helping out. I was already such a big help that everyone took it for granted that I would help. I knew how to help. I was forever watching the twins. I was singing to them, rocking them and putting them to sleep. I loved them it was like they were my dolls. I would dress them and clean them. When I wasn't taking care of the baby's Mother would put me up to the sink on a chair and have me wash dishes. Mother instructed me early on how to do the dishes. I washed the dishes. I rinsed and dried them. Then I put them away in the cupboard. I would sweep the floor. I hung out the laundry. I folded the laundry at least the small things. I didn't realize the enormity of the job I would be taking on. God did though that is why he allowed me to do the things I did. That is why he gave me instructions early on. He knew that pretty soon I would need these fleeting moments of helping my mother. Memories of my mother to sustain me through a life time of hurt.

With all these children to take care of no one seemed to butt into our business. What was going on inside the house on

South Harris Avenue? If the neighbors cared enough they didn't show it. We even had the Post Master General of our local Post Office and his wife lived across the street. They didn't like it but they didn't stop it either. No one could stop the abuse. If they did try to stop the abuse the beatings got a whole lot more severe. My mother ran away several times. Our Dad came and got her, dragging her and all of us kids back home. Those people who harbored us were in trouble. It would start all over again.

It started a deep seeded hatred in me for my dad. It would take years to recover from. God tells us to love our parents. When I saw all this abuse it was hard for me to believe in the things from Sunday school. I didn't know how to love my dad. All he ever taught me was to hate him. I was confused. How do I love a man like this? He was not only destroying my mother physically but mentally. He was destroying her and her self-respect. Little by little chip by chip he was also destroying each and every one of his children's self-respect. We were too afraid to gang up on him for fear of hurting our mother and all of us more. We didn't understand how God could expect us to love someone like this?

Just hearing weren't enough you had to be an eye witness to experience the full measure of the agony.

Day in and day out it was the same. All the screaming! If it was possible my nerves were always shattered. I never knew from one day to the next who was going to be mad at whom? Who was going to get who riled up? There was never any peace. From morning till night Dad was always drinking too!

Today is my birthday.

I turned 4 years old today.

No one remembered.

Mom and Dad's marriage

In 1940, my parents, Ella Loree Lamb and Arthur Charles Baas were married. He was a full blooded German. She was a mix of a lot of different nationalities. One of Grandma Baas's biggest contentions against our mother was that she was a country bumpkin without a home of her own.

One of Ella's great-grandmothers was a full-blooded American Indian.

Needless to say that didn't sit well with the full-blooded German's mother. My Grandma Frieda felt Ella was not good enough for her son. She was not going to allow her son to marry a half breed. My Dad was twenty-five. He married Ella against the wishes of his parents. Ella was only sixteen and still in high school. Six weeks from graduation. She quit school to get married. Her mother didn't like it any better than his mother. Heck she thought he was too old. She felt he was taking advantage of her daughter.

Shortly after the secret ceremony my Grandma Baas took Ella to the doctor's. Grandma Baas wanted to make sure my mother didn't have any diseases. Also she didn't want grandchildren from this union. So she had the doctors implant a device into Ella so she would not have children.

After a little time passed and mother still wasn't pregnant. Dad started asking questions about it. Mother said, "Your mother took me to the doctor. She had a device implanted to keep me from getting pregnant with your children." Dad was furious. What right did she have to interfere? He had wanted kids right away. He was tired of his mothers' interference. So he yanked the device out of my mother. My mother ended up in the hospital because of the hemorrhaging. My mother could have died because of my dad's temper.

My dad was the oldest child. His mother continuously interfered in his life. Dad wanted to go to college for music and pay for it himself. His parents told him what kind of music he would play. He could not go anywhere or do anything without his mother's okay. He was a grown man. She was still trying to interfere in his life. He hated it. His cousins and the guys at school always called him a mama's boy. He hated this too.

His parents told him he couldn't go to college until he helped to pay for the college of his younger brother first. Then the both of them would pay for my dad's college. Well my dad did pay for his younger brother to go to college but he never got to go. His younger brother wouldn't help him. Dad's parents never made the younger brother follow through. Dad did not think that was fair.

Dad was even offered a job with a prominent Jazz band. He was in his twenties. His parents said, "No!" They wouldn't allow him to take this job. The entertainment world did not have a good reputation. They wanted their son to play only hymns. He liked jazz. My dad put his violin away and never got it out again. On rare occasions he would bring out his violin. He was very good.

Dad had saved up a lot of money from his jobs. He paid cash for a house. He bought my mother a house as a wedding present. It was a nice two bedrooms, two story Cape Cod with a crawl space. Our dad and one of our uncles helped him to do a little bit of painting and remodeling. My mother (as a child) lived with other family members because her mother was a single mother (widow) without a home of her own. So my mother was very excited about having a house of her own.

The first thing they did was put an archway between the living room and dining room. They wanted both rooms to appear bigger than they were. It was a very small house. It was in a really nice neighborhood. Nice home for a newlywed and a growing family. They were excited about having a home of their own.

They had an L shaped porch around the west and the south side of the house. It was a white house with a huge picture window in front where the living room was. It had two side windows as well, one in the living room and one in the dining room.

The first thing my mother did was add a porch swing. Then she put a lilac bush right outside the window of the kitchen. During the springtime when the wind would blow you could smell the lilacs when they were in bloom. Their house had a back porch which was very large. They were so happy with their new home.

The thing my dad was most happy about with their new house was that it had a two car garage in the back. He was already tinkering with fixing cars. His passion was cars. Something he would teach all his boys later on.

They didn't have a bunch of furniture. They had two couches in the living room. One on each side, the north side which was a hide a bed (sofa bed) and the south side couch was a davenport. It could be turned into a bed. They also had a rocking chair so that mother could rock her babies as she had them. In the dining room they had a buffet on the north side with a matching formal dining room table and chairs. The kitchen had a gas stove and a refrigerator (ice box). It also had a kitchen table with chairs. Later as the family grew dad would make a bench. Off the kitchen was a bathroom.

Dad was drafted into the Army to fight in World War Two. He wanted to go after the bombing of Pearl Harbor. I think all the men wanted to go, just like with 9/11. Dad and mother were glad they had bought her a house. A lot of wives had to scramble to find a place to live while their men were off fighting in the war. But she had a house and didn't have to worry about where she was going to live.

My mother volunteered at the Red Cross and at the Moose Lodge to help our fighting men. Her own fighting man too.

My oldest brother was born 1942 Art Jr. The first grandchild for both sides of the family always gets spoiled don't they?

Dad got one leave during his time in the Army. He was allowed to come home for one twenty-four hour session. Guess what? My mother got pregnant with baby number two a girl. She was eight months old when our dad came home from the Army. He was hurt pretty bad with shrapnel in the brain. He and one other man was the only ones left alive in his whole platoon. The other soldiers had all been killed. He himself lay in a pool of his own blood for more than twenty-four hours before help arrived, He said, "there were bodies all around him." He almost died.

Dad did live through the ordeal. When he came home he came home to an eighteen month old daughter and a four year old son. Neither one of these two children knew who this man was.

I don't know where dad went to recuperate from his wounds. He never talked about that part of his life. Every once in a while I would get a glimpse of what it must have been like for him over there in Germany during the war. He was a mechanic on the heavy equipment and vehicles. He loved what he did so much he brought the skills home and opened his own business as a mechanic. He was pretty good too. He managed to get a few good contracts. He got the city fleet of police cars. He also got the mayor's car as part of his contract until the city got too big and they decided to hire their own mechanics.

Dad's time in the army had changed him and not for the better. He was moody all the time. He was drinking and smoking heavily. He would no sooner put out a cigarette when he lit another one. It seemed like that was all the military wanted to do was to pass out cigarettes and beer. Yes the military made him start drinking heavily. He never seemed to be without a beer or a cigarette.

Life during the War

While dad was away at the war, Mother had many trials too. How to stretch the money there was very little. This is where her mother came in handy. Grandma Lamb was a nurse's aide so she also earned a small salary. My mother was a stay-at-home mother most women didn't work back then. My mother was one of the lucky ones. Her husband paid cash for their house. She didn't have to worry about making a house payment just utilities and groceries.

Mother almost lost her life during this time. While she was canning vegetables from the small vegetable garden she always had, one of the jars burst open inside the pressure cooker. Mother reached in to get out the jar (after it had cooled down) she cut her hand severely. She had cut a main artery in her wrist. She wasn't found until Grandma Lamb came home from work and by that time she had almost bled to death.

Dad had his own trials during the war as well. A lot of his buddies received "Dear John" letters. Why these letters always seemed to get through while hardly any of the good letters got through still mystifies me. Some of the letters never got home until the end of the war.

Also no one knew dad had almost lost his life more than once.

Like most soldiers that had seen real action, Dad rarely talked about his time in Germany.

The one time I recall him telling the most was the time where he and only one of his buddies lived through a battle. He had spent the next twenty-four hours waiting for help to arrive. He couldn't holler out just in case the Germans were still there. He lay in the rain, the mud and in the blood among all those corpses. Some of them were his buddies. He was the only one around for miles that lived. It was not until much later after he was taken to the hospital that he was told one of his buddies had made it also. He was sent home after this with a piece of shrapnel still lodged in his brain.

It was a cold wintery blustery day when dad arrived back on the home front. He came by way of the bus system. It was not very reliable at best. He just happened to get on one of the buses that did not run very well. It broke down out in the middle of nowhere. The bus driver did not know what to do. He knew he did not have enough fuel to keep all the passengers warm. He also knew if he called the dispatchers office it would be hours before help could arrive. The bus driver also knew how poor communication was. We didn't have wireless phones back then. He didn't have any alternatives but to call and get help. He was about to do just that when my dad spoke up and said he would take a look at the bus. He told the driver that heavy equipment was his specialty in the army. A bus couldn't be any worse than any of the artillery he worked on. My Dad said, "The bus driver looked doubtful but let him give it a try. He didn't have anything to lose go ahead." It took dad almost an hour to fix it but fix it he did. My Dad had been a heavy utilities mechanic during the war. So he knew how to fix just about anything that had wheels on it. The army taught him that.

A lot of the other passengers were service men like my dad. They were all quite impressed. He was the hero that day.

That evening dad arrived home. The first person to greet him was a girl-child. He knew of a son but not of a daughter. The first words he said were, "This is not my child. Get this child out of my sight."

Vera had never met a man before. She started screaming at the top of her lungs. Dad could not believe that this child was his. He had not been home long enough on his last leave for this to have happened. He could not believe any woman could have been faithful the whole time. A lot of his buddies received "Dear John" letters.

This first sight of each other was to be the scene that would be replayed throughout most of Vera's childhood.

Mother had been faithful to dad but he never believed her. Vera was the result of his leave during the war.

Grandma Lamb was there that night. She had spent many nights with mother while dad was away. Dad immediately started hitting mother for her unfaithfulness. The war had taken its toll on Dad. Mother got the brunt of it. The military was served beer day in and day out. There wasn't any clean water available. Needless to say Grandma's and dad's relationship deteriorated rapidly.

Grandma had heard all the accusations about her daughter and her granddaughter. She was pretty upset he accused her daughter of cheating on him. She wouldn't take her son-in-law hurting either of them. Grandma told my dad, "If you don't like the way things were run get out now. We don't need you around here stirring up trouble. I will not tolerate you hitting my daughter or granddaughter."

Well that sobered Dad up quite a bit. He could not believe his mother-in-law was talking to him this way in his own house.

Dad hollered back, "old woman if you don't like the way I run things you get. It's my house. Get out now! I will not tolerate any woman telling me what to do in my own house.'

Next dad asked, "Where is Jr.?" With this Grandma said, "At your mother's house. She never did feel Ella was good enough for you. After you left she took Jr. with her to protect him. Imagine her thinking Ella is not good enough for you. It is you who is not good enough for Ella. It is your mother who is nothing but a busy body. She does nothing but stir up trouble. Your mother gets into other people's business when she shouldn't. She always has"

"Shut up old woman" shouted Art, "or I will hit you too. I have had a hard day."

They continued to bicker back and forth a lot. Grandma was furious that dad could accuse her daughter of being unfaithful. After everything she had endured throughout the whole pregnancy, and the war and she told him as much.

When Vera was born you could see exactly whose daughter she was. Grandma resented the fact that he could deny the paternity of this child. She helped to watch this child every day and had come to love her more and more.

Dad left to go to his mother's house to get Jr. However what Dad found at his mother's didn't sit well with him either. His own mother argued with him to not take Jr. with him. "Whose child do you think he is yours?" Dad refused to negotiate on this matter. His mother had no right to take Jr. away in the first place. He felt his mother had already done enough damage and told her as much. My Grandpa stepped in and returned Jr. to my Dad. This rift lasted years. Grandma Baas had done irreparable damage to his son's relationship to his own mother.

When Dad arrived home with Jr. in tow the first person who greeted Jr. was a little girl. It did not take Jr. long to realize that this little girl was his little sister. Jr. was furious. Immediately he felt his mother couldn't have loved him to have left him at his other grandma's house. She let his little sister stay with her. Jr. didn't realize that it was not his mother's idea. It was the manipulations of Grandma Baas that had caused this.

Grandma Baas thought girls were useless. That is why she didn't take Vera too. She wanted nothing to do with little girls. She even said as much to anyone who would listen. They were good for cleaning and having babies.

Jr. immediately saw Vera as his rival, a rivalry that would last a very long time. Jr. started saying things, "Grandma Baas loves me more than you." Vera would say things like "So what Grandma Lamb loves me more than you. Mother too cause I got to stay with them and you didn't."

Through no fault of their own they became enemies because of family interference.

No one understood Jr.'s resentment or bitterness of his sister and his mother. Mother and Dad were too busy trying to get to know each other again to even realize there was a problem.

It didn't take Jr. very long to see there was a strain between his dad and sister. Instead of him trying to make friends with Vera he started teasing her. He told his sister dad didn't love her and his Grandma Baas didn't love her either. The lines were drawn each child trying to irritate the other with their own special Grandma. This scene was played back and forth throughout their childhood and into adulthood. Neither one of the Grandma's had time for any of the other children. Before they were even brother and sister they were rivals. Dad claiming Vera was not his child also reinforced this rivalry. I remember hearing them as teenagers arguing which grandma was whose and which grandma loved who more.

Jr. continued to feel that his mother did not love him. He began to follow in his Dad's footsteps. Everywhere dad went Jr. went also. Of course mother loved Jr., she was not a forceful person. She was very meek and mild mannered. Everyone kept thinking he would outgrow it, he never did.

Grandma Baas was a law unto herself. She did what she wanted when she wanted. There were a lot of times that Grandpa stepped in and put his foot down to curtail her busy body activities. So when grandma had a chance to do something she did it with a vengeance. Jr. was not to know these things though. He just felt unwanted and unloved by his mother.

Jr. did not have far to go to tag along with dad. He would get up with dad. Go to work with dad. Then go home with dad. The garage was behind the house. Dad thought it was cute his little grease monkey. Jr. thought that if his mother did not love him maybe dad would. He knew dad did not care a thing for Vera. He knew also that dad had even claimed Vera was not his child. So he wanted to have someone like Vera had mother. He wanted to hurt Vera like he was hurt.

Jr. never knew how much his mother loved him. He harbored his own ill feelings towards his sister and his mother all his life. He let it eat away at him never healing.

The Family Grows and Grows and Grows

In November of 1946, Mother gave birth to her third child. This was the first child dad had seen from infancy. Dad was with our mother throughout the whole pregnancy. He was ecstatic. Most people think this was the reason she became dad's favorite. But it was this and much, more.

They named her Karen. Mother had a hard delivery. The nurse's wanted to wait until the doctor came to deliver the baby. But the baby had other ideas. Twice Karen started down the delivery canal. Twice the nurse pushed her back inside. When the baby was pushed back in the second time, Mother began to scream. Dad and Grandma Lamb heard the screams and went to the rescue. They shoved the nurse out of the way and delivered the baby themselves before the doctor arrived. Grandma Lamb had helped deliver babies before so she and dad delivered this one too.

They were afraid some minor brain damage might have been done to this child by the nurse. This is just another reason for the closeness that existed between dad and his third child.

Karen was the first child Dad heard say her first words. She was the first one he saw take her first steps. This also brought mother and dad closer together. It began healing the rift that had been growing between them because of the two older kids and the war. World War II separated many families back then.

Both Jr. and Vera saw Karen as a threat. So they started resenting her. For the first time in Jr.'s and Vera's, life they worked together to solve the problem of their younger sister. Karen was getting all the attention they felt they deserved. Neither one realizing the baby needed more attention than they did. They only saw Karen as someone to take away something of theirs, their parents. No one tried to tell them differently. My parents were too busy with a growing family and healing their own wounds to see what was happening right under their noses.

With all this love and devotion showered on her, Karen became a very loving child. She was able to give love and show love. Karen had dark blond hair, blue eyes and looked a lot like dad. She smiled all the time. She was a happy baby.

Jr. and Vera felt they were being cheated. Jr. always seemed to wear a scowl on his face. He had brown hair, blue eyes, and really curly hair, to the point of being unruly. Vera had a constant smirk on her face. Like she was always looking for ways to get even with you and she usually did. She had dark blond hair and blue eyes.

Jr. and Vera resented Karen for these things. Karen's every wish was granted. Dad's love for Karen seemed to even surpass his love for his own wife. Karen felt guilty. She tried to make up for this lack, which was not her fault. However mother saw Karen as her way to get a few things that she needed or wanted for the house. Karen was very obliging, and did as mother asked. She became the liaison to our dad. If anyone ever needed something they asked Karen to ask dad to get it. If Karen asked Dad, he said, "Yes."

As Karen grew older the resentments of her older brother and sister grew more severe. They joined forces against their little sister to make her life miserable. They would pull out her hair. Take away her toys. Every chance they got. One day they had pulled out so much of her hair she was totally bald. If she would have squealed on them Jr. and Vera it would have been worse. She didn't need to tell their parents they knew anyway. Mom and dad didn't do anything at first.

After it got really severe these pranks played on Karen our parents got really mad. When our parents found out about these little games, the older ones played on Karen they would get a spanking. This made Jr. and Vera resent Karen all the more.

Jr's. resentments grew and simmered just below the surface. He became our dad's little grease monkey. He knew it was the one time when he would get dad to himself. Then dad began to expect it of him. It was no longer fun. Dad became very dependent upon Jr., as his assistant in every way and without pay. The resentment he harbored was getting wider and wider. He loved his father. He loved his mother. But Jr. could not help feeling resentment to them both.

There were too many children for our mother to stop and notice. One of her young ones was harboring such feelings of resentment. Jr. was never around her long enough for her to notice these things about him. When she did finally notice she didn't know how to help him. Her mother in law had taken control of Jr. during the war. He came home at the age of four. She could do nothing to change that. If he would have given her a chance she would have tried to do something. Jr. didn't want her help. The resentment he felt for her for never coming for him was already burning. He didn't know she didn't have a driver's license to drive and get him. Jr. did not know she could not drive.

Vera, being the oldest girl had to help mother a lot. She resented this every bit as much as Jr. resented helping dad. Both felt if mother and dad would not have any more kids they might get more of their parent's attention. But mother and dad did have more kids.

After Karen was born it was two and a half years before there was another child born. This child was a boy. My parents named him Larry. This was the first boy born to our parents after the war. He became the favorite boy. He and Karen became very close for protection. Then every eighteen months after that there was another child born. It was never again like it was with Karen and Larry. The remaining eleven children were born between

1951 and 1958 a total of seven more children. There was one miscarriage as well in 1957.

It literally got too busy to harbor resentments. They were still there. Just barely below the surface waiting for an opportunity to erupt. With some the explosion occurred. With others the explosion is still waiting just below the surface waiting to erupt. It is eating away at all their feelings. The feelings they could have for anyone or anything else including themselves.

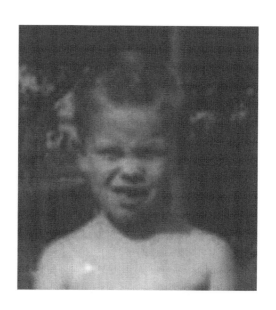

Dad Ain't Gonna Whip Me No More

Throughout the hardships there were some funny times too. At least our parents thought they were funny. My brother John was a pistol. He never out grew the prank-ster stag. His went beyond just ordinary pranks. His were mean and cruel. But still our dad would not punish him. He just stood around and bragged about his esca-pades. Dad thought they were hilarious. Mostly it was dad and Grandma Lamb who did the bragging about John. Our mother didn't think it was all that funny. She thought it was downright cruel for them to encourage such behavior.

John was the fifth child. He had blond hair, blue eyes and curly unruly hair. He was always smiling. It was a cruel smile. The smile never entered his eyes. As he grew he developed an attitude. He was always in fights at school. He became a bully at home and at school.

One time when John was around three years old dad gave John a whipping. He did something he was not supposed to be doing. Well John had a mind of his own. Come hell or high water he was bound and determined to do it his way. Just like dad. They were two peas in a pod. John mimicked dad so much it was uncanny. By the results one would think it was dad who had done the prank. But you would see for yourself that it was John and you had to believe.

After John's whipping he got a twinkle in his eye and a smile on his face you knew he was up to no good. But no one paid any attention to him. They figured he'd be good for a little while. Right! Wrong! Dad had just finished whipping him for being bad. They temporarily forgot that John had a mind of his own. A spanking didn't faze him one bit. So while no one was watching him he went outside. If someone had seen the determined look in his eyes they would have watched him. They didn't and they were sorry for it later. But you see John was just spanked. It was not a light tap either. Dad went back to sleep where he had been just before he had whipped John. He and Mother slept on the hide-a-couch in the living room. In a two bedroom home with eight kids you slept where you could. This arrangement gave the parents easy access to the kids and vice-versa us kids easy access to our parents.

John came back into the house. If anyone had seen him then they would have known he was definitely up to no good.

But they didn't.

John was chanting and skipping.

John's chant was,

"Dad ain't gonna whip me no more!"

"Dad ain't gonna whip me no more!"

"Dad ain't gonna whip me no more!"

"Dad ain't gonna whip me no more!"

The whole time he was saying this chant everyone heard. No one paid any attention. John was carrying a cement cinder block. He was skipping through the house. He went all the way into the living room this way. As he stood over our dad he raised this cement block. There was a smile on his face and he chanted softly, one last time

"Dad ain't gonna whip me no more!" John dropped the cement block on dad's head. The noise it made could be heard all over the house. Then there was a grunt as if someone was in pain. Then everyone saw what was going on. They remembered the chant that John had been saying. They realized John had been quite serious that dad would never whip him again. He was trying to get rid of his own dad at three years old.

Dad was knocked out. He was unconscious for quite a while. John did get another whipping. Exactly what he said dad wouldn't do again. The problem was yes they would whip him. Then they turned right around and brag about his escapades. This didn't make any sense to me at all. They actually thought it was funny. The only thing was his antics progressively got worse.

It would take quite an imaginative child to come up with such an idea, all on his own. It is just too bad he didn't have his imagination channeled in some other direction. Instead he was allowed to do mean little trouble making pranks. He was quite unique in his antics, he was an original.

As John grew older his antics just seemed to get worse. Until eventually John became uncontrollable. But that is another story.

I am telling this story to let you see how each one of us was treated differently throughout our young lives. It seemed there wasn't any rhyme or reason to it. Some were treated like they could do no wrong while others were treated as if they could do nothing right.

Dad always told John, "You don't have to listen to your mother! You don't have to listen to your teachers! You don't have to listen to your older sister's even if they are babysitting you! Women do not matter." So John grew up with this attitude. Women were useless. They did not matter. They did not count. Only boys counted and mattered! Girls were good for cooking, cleaning, having babies and taking care of the man.

John was eighteen months older than me. We were the same height he had blonde hair and blue eyes like our dad. He always wore a buzz haircut. That was the style for boys back then. He didn't respect women. Our dad taught him this. He walked with a swagger. He dared anyone to cross his path. At school he was known as the class bully. All the kids at school were afraid of him. John didn't take any crap from anyone. No adult or teachers could make John do anything. He was always being sent down to the principal's office for some kind of incident or other.

Then he would brag about it to our dad. They would both laugh about it later.

I became John's punching bag. I looked like mother. Mother was our dad's punching bag. So John copied dad. So every time I turned around and no one was looking I got punched in the stomach. No one saw John hit me. He made sure of this. I was always crying it hurt. I hated it. I was always being hit or punched and then John didn't get the blame - I did. They would ask me, "What did you do to make John hit you?" They never once asked John to stop. They never once asked him why he picked on me. As John turned his back on the adults I saw the smirk on his face. It just didn't make any sense. I was the good one. I didn't do anything to make John mad. John just liked to hit things. He just needed someone to take his frustration out on. I just happen to be the thing he chose. I cried and was sad a lot. If there wasn't already enough turmoil in our lives we had to endure things like this as well.

I did get even with John though. It took a while and that is in another story because I was a lot older and stronger then.

As we grew John was not the only one who grew. I grew too. I grew smarter too. One day I took my head and acted like a bull. I took my head and full force hit John in the stomach. My parents were not going to protect me I was going to protect myself. I did it the only way I knew. John doubled over in pain. I had knocked the wind out of him. He quit picking on me for a while he was much more careful.

The Christmas Train

Christmas was always special. It was a magical time of year at our house. It was one of the few times of the year my dad was sober.

There was a tin train placed carefully on the tracks around the Christmas tree. The whistle would blow, the smoke stack would actually smoke and the light on the front of the engine would light up. The train would run merrily and happily around the Christmas tree. It would run through the Christmas village as if it didn't have a care in the world. It was like the train took on a life of its own. You would watch it go around and around. The whistle blew and the smoke stack blew some more. We would pretend it was picking up passengers. We would be the passengers. It was taking us to some place special where bad things didn't happen to little kids. As the train went around the tracks you would watch as if mesmerized. Pretending this world of broken promises and dreams didn't exist. There was only this magical world of Christmas. A place where there is not any pain and a place where kids could be kids.

We were allowed to play with all the decorations. The older children and the middle children taught the younger ones how to play with the trinkets and toys. So that they wouldn't get broken or damaged and we could continue to play with them. Never thinking of what tomorrow would bring. My Dad called them trinkets and toys instead of ornaments. These moments had to be remembered again and again to last until next Christmas. But as long as this Christmas lasted we were very careful to not break even one piece. Just by breaking one little piece we would break the spell of the magic of this Christmas.

You see my Dad was an alcoholic. During the Christmas season, from Christmas Eve to New Year's Day he was sober. He did not drink during this time. It was like he was trying to make up for all the things he had done wrong throughout the whole year. He pretended that everything was different that he was different. He promised to never get drunk again. We all believed him. We wanted something to believe in. We tried to pretend and pray that he was actually different too. We tried to forget that it may just be a show he put on every year.

I loved Christmas because Dad was sober and because he made it special for all of us.

But not everyone loved Christmas. My oldest sister Vera hated Christmas. She hated everything about Christmas. She hated setting up the tree. She hated not being allowed to go to bed to sleep. She was one of the older ones and they had to stay up late to help decorate the tree. They had to help wrap presents for the younger brothers and sisters. She hated them too because there were just too many of us.

She felt she always had to watch them. She hated that too. There wasn't one thing about Christmas that made her happy.

Dad had to practically make her do things in order for her to help set up the tree. It was finally left up to Karen, Larry and Jr. to help set up the tree. Vera would just sit on the couch and sulk with her arms folded across her chest. She wished she was one of the lucky ones. She just wanted to go to bed. She wanted to make this nightmare of a night end. We (the younger ones and I) always thought she was one of the lucky ones. We the younger ones couldn't wait until we were old enough to help. We wanted to help decorate the tree. The very thing she detested we wanted to do. So Vera resented Christmas. She hated the fact that she had to stay up most of the night. She hated putting up the tree for her ungrateful little bratty brothers and sisters. She always told us, "If mom and dad hadn't had so many children then we could do more things. They should have stopped having children a long time ago." Grandma Baas used to say this all the time as well. That Mother and Dad just had too many children was Grandma Baas's excuse for not visiting us very often.

So for Vera all the Christmases came and went. The magic that was Christmas for the rest of us passed her by altogether. Nothing anyone said or did could make my oldest sister Vera feel any better. All of us younger kids would be so excited. We would be oohing and aahing over our presents. She would spoil it all by saying, "it is only because I stayed up late. I had to wrap everything myself to make any of this possible." So even for us younger ones she tried to spoil our fun. No one was even the wiser. We were too afraid of her to tell anyone. We did not know any better than to think she had done it all herself. She was trying to give us a guilt trip.

The tin train wasn't even magical for Vera. She wouldn't even let us feel excited about watching the smoke stack on the train engine. Nor would she allow us to enjoy the engine sounds. Nor would she allow us to enjoy the lights on the engine. But when her back was turned we would watch anyway. A light would shine in our eyes that could not be taken away. It was there for all to see if you looked carefully enough. To us it was a new beginning. A new season of fun and laughter which Vera could not understand? She would sulk and sleep the whole day away. She would wish for Christmas to be gone. She wished for Dad to go back to work as if nothing had ever happened. Then she could go about business as usual and not be bothered anymore. She did not see the things we saw.

But the magic of Christmas could never be taken away from us. It would be locked away in our hearts and minds until we needed a time to remember the good days. God knew we would need a time to remember how happy we were at Christmas. God also knew we needed to remember how much fun we had pretending we were the little passengers on the magical Christmas Train. All of my younger brothers and sisters loved Christmas too. They loved it when we told them stories about the magic of Christmas. We taught the younger ones how to play with the trinkets and toys without breaking them. They loved every minute of Christmas too. They too under stood without being told that breaking just one of these precious little gems would break the spell and the magic of the Christmas.

Dad would put Christmas music on the record player and we would all sit around and sing Christmas carols. We would laugh and sing and unwrap presents. There weren't too many presents, just two or three items each. But when you have so many children you don't need to have a lot of presents for the living room to look full of presents. Mother always made doll clothes for all of our dolls. I don't know how she found the time with all the children she had. Trying to cook and clean for us all she still managed to find the time. It was a lot of fun to have new doll clothes for your doll under the tree. The material wasn't new. Even the dolls got hand me downs. Their clothes were made out of all our worn out clothes. But it was new to us. We always got socks and underwear too. Mother was the best at making something out of nothing. She loved making us happy. We all loved her for it.

Sunday School

My deep faith in God helped me to cope with all the abuse I was receiving. What helped my faith to grow stronger were my Sunday school teachers. They taught me that God was a loving God. That He sent His son Jesus for me. He loved me that much. His son died for my sins. His son loved me that much. His son's name was Jesus. I loved Him for loving me. I wasn't exactly sure I understood what sinning was. I didn't think I understood it completely but it did make me feel special. It made me feel good. It made me feel good that Jesus loved me this much. It made me feel good that somebody loved me.

The Sunday school teachers told of the good stories of the Bible. They told of Joseph and his coat of many colors. They even gave me a felt picture with Joseph's coat on it. It was beautiful. I would go home and tell these stories to my younger brothers and sisters. Some of them were not old enough to attend Sunday school. There were so many good stories to hear and retell. I used to write plays about these stories. I would make my younger brothers and sisters into the actors and actresses. I told them how they should act. Where they were to stand and I was the narrator. They loved to help me make the stories. We would put on plays for the neighborhood kids too to earn money. We never made any money but we gave it a really good effort.

Then we would sing beautiful songs like "Jesus loves me", "Zacchaeus was a Wee Little Man", "Jacob's ladder", and "Kumbaya" just to name a few. Beautiful songs that I still love to sing today.

The Christmas Programs were the best. I was allowed to be in them. I either sang or had a speaking part when I was younger. I loved the manger scenes with baby Jesus. I was even an angel once. It was a lot of fun. It took my mind off the stresses at home. The other kids were kind to me. The teachers seemed to like me. I just loved the Christmas plays.

After all the festivities and the program was over all the kids got a special present. One of the things we got was a whole box of chocolate drops. I ate some of them on the way home. The rest I would share with the younger brothers and sisters who were not old enough to go. They were delicious. To this day old fashioned chocolate drops bring back very fond memories of my childhood Christmas programs. They are hard to find these days but every Christmas I search the stores until I find them.

The songs in the Christmas programs were wonderful too. Songs like "Away in a Manger", and "O Little Town of Bethlehem".

But the best thing that happened when I was at church was the singing. Our children's choir director liked me. She was a great singer. She also had a daughter named Carmen. Carmen had the voice of an angel. It must have been passed down by her mother. Carmen's mother always had me sitting or standing next to her daughter. So as I grew I heard Carmen's voice singing in my ear. Every time we practiced and sang. My voice grew too. I learned to sing. I learned to hear music in my ear. I learned to hear music in my head. I didn't understand the enormity of the gift I was receiving. The choir director was giving me quite a gift by letting me stand next to her daughter. I thank God every day for this beautiful blessed gift he allowed me to have. I still love to sing.

Carmen and I were the same age. She was beautiful. She had dark brown almost black hair that sparkled when the dazzling sunlight hit it. She had dark brown eyes and long eye lashes. She was quiet like I was. She was as beautiful on the inside. Carmen didn't mind that I sat next to her. If she did mind she never showed it. I wore tatty clothes too. I must have had a smell too but I didn't know I stank. Both of my parents smoked a lot. I smelled of unwashed body odor.

We weren't allowed to talk in church or during choir practice. I felt special just sitting next to her. She had beautiful clothes. Her parents only had two children. Her dad was the High School Band Director. Music was in her blood. He was teaching my oldest sister Vera to play the violin.

What was given to me in this way couldn't be taken away from me by any adult. My singing made me happy. It made me feel good inside. Any time I was sad I was singing or humming or whistling even if it was only in my head. I never ever forgot what a special blessing I had received. To this day singing keeps me free from stress.

Singing was my favorite subject I learned to love music. I loved all the hymns at church. I sang them loud too because the songs made me feel good inside and out.

It would be much later when I would learn the full benefit of what was given to me at church in my Sunday school classrooms.

Halloween, And Other Holidays

Another favorite season of mine was Halloween. Dad always came home early. He came home before the trick or treaters set out with their bags or pillow cases for carrying their loot. With Dad getting home early there wasn't nearly as much time for getting stinking drunk. He wanted to be the first to be able to eat candy. He would even stop by the store and picked up candy to pass out to the trick r treaters. We always had a blast. We were bums, hobos, or ghosts. This way it didn't cost any money. We had the natural grease from Dad's auto mechanics shop. We started going trick or treating as soon as it was dark. It was a lot of fun trying to see who could get the most candy. It seemed to last all evening long well past bedtime. I always tried to keep up with Larry and John but they were just too fast. I would try even harder till I got hurt by running into things. It seemed like John and Larry always got the most candy and the biggest candy bars. Naturally I wanted a piece of the action. I was never successful because they didn't want their bratty little sister coming with them.

When I wasn't trying to keep up with the big kids and went at my own pace I did get a lot of candy. There were tons of decorations. Everyone had carved pumpkins with candles inside. Almost everyone had ghosts hanging from their porch. Everywhere you looked there were porches. Everyone sat on the porches to pass out the candy when it was warm. But when it wasn't warm, we had to ring the doorbell then we had to say, "trick or treat." Almost everyone passed out candy but there were some who didn't like Halloween. They just said, "Go on get out of here. That's a trick for you."

No one warned us of the dangers of Halloween that someone might steal our candy. These were different times. The kids didn't have to worry about kidnappings. We were allowed to have fun for a change. We stayed out till well after dark. It usually took a good couple of hours. There were a lot of houses between Sullivant Avenue and Broad Street.

We ran as fast our legs would take us and it was fun. It was freedom without a care in the world. John and Larry taught us that if we held back a little we could see what kind of candy they were passing out. We hit only the houses that were passing out the big candy bars. I think that is why all of us younger ones wanted to follow them. We wanted to learn the tricks of the trade.

When we got home however it was different. Dad opened up our candy bags and peeked inside. He reached inside the bag. He dumped each bag individually on the floor. Dad took all of the favorite candy bars and the biggest candy bars. He took all the Butterfingers, Babe Ruths, and Hershey bars then he hid them. So if you didn't eat any while you were out trick or treating you didn't get even one. I looked everywhere couldn't find them. Dad ate them. John and Larry knew this. So they went through their bags themselves and hid their best candy bars before Dad could get any. This got Dad mad and he asked them where their big candy bars were. They said in unison: "We didn't get any." I don't think Dad believed them but he didn't say anything to them.

In the morning when Dad got up and went to work he took his loot with him. He was afraid someone would get into his stash of candy. He had taken ours. He was probably right. Dad ended up ruining our fun again on Halloween again by taking all the best candy.

Easter wasn't much better. Dad and Mom would buy Easter candy for all of us.

We would wake up Easter morning and have Easter baskets. The Easter Bunny had left them for us. Dad would go through these Easter baskets and take all of the best chocolates. Even before I got one piece of the malted milk balls he had most of them gone.

We did get to color Easter eggs. This was fun. Every one of us who wanted to color eggs could color about a dozen. This was fun. We all tried to see who could make the prettiest? Who could make the ugliest egg? Who would make the most original egg? When they were all colored and decorated we just sat back and admired our handy work. We all thought we had done the best or the most. No one ever really knew who did the best. All we heard from our Mother was, "you all did the best."

After we opened our Easter baskets we got dressed and went to church. To get all of us ready for church was a chore. We started getting ready the night before. So every Saturday night became get ready for church night. Mother got all the shoes out to make sure they were polished. They were all lined up in a row in the dining room underneath the window or underneath the buffet. After this task was done she made sure we all had socks. The socks were put inside the shoe so no one could say that is my sock. Then she made sure all of us had a clean outfit to wear. It was quite a challenge.

We went to Sunday school first. Then we went to church. Mother made sure we went to church on Easter. Everybody went. Dad even made a point to go to church on Easter Sunday. The ladies of the church usually served Easter breakfast in between Sunday school and church service. My dad was not going to miss out on free food for all of us.

After church we usually went to my Grandma Baas's house for dinner. She also had her other children and grandchildren there. Goodness gracious that is a lot of people. My dad had eleven children. One of his brothers had five children. My dad's sister had three children. My dad's other brother had two. Grandma made Easter baskets for all her grandchildren. Her favorite grandchildren got bigger baskets. We always got the smallest baskets.

Grandma always had an Easter egg hunt. This was fun. It made it seem more normal. It made it seem like she liked us a little even if it was for show. We were made to sit on the couch or on the floor. We were not allowed to mingle with our cousins or our aunts and uncles. If we moved Grandpa would crack us over the head with his cane. It hurt. We were afraid of Grandpa.

Nightmares

After witnessing Mother's attack I had nightmares. Not only while I was asleep but they seemed to continue into my waking hours as well. I was very skittish. I was afraid of my own shadow. I could not look anyone in the eye. I was afraid they would see I was frightened. I could not talk to anyone about it. Who would I talk to? I couldn't sleep at night.

The nights were the worst. All night long we heard the screams from the bathroom. Now I knew why? It would have been better if I didn't know why? We would cover our ears with our pillows. But the screams were still there. We tried to cover our ears to block out the noise but the screams could still be heard. It seemed like that is the way the nights went. You would finally fall sleep only to be awakened by more screams. Except these screams were your very own screams. You were screaming for someone to leave you alone and to not touch you. Screaming because there was blood everywhere and you just couldn't get away from it.

Summertime, with the opened windows was the worst. The sounds seemed to go straight out of the bathroom window and into the upstairs bedroom window. I was so afraid of the bathroom. At night I couldn't go to the bathroom. I had to hold my pee all night long. It felt like some nights it started right after supper. It went on into the wee hours of the morning. Sometimes I would go down to the basement to use the drain hole down there. The sewer drain hole. You believed that you didn't have any choice in the matter. But then the older brothers and sisters found out. They watched and waited until you were at a critical point than they would scare the daylights out of us. They did this to all of their younger brothers and sisters, not just me. They would scream or make sounds of wild animals. They would do it at just the right point when it was time to do your potty business. I was a pretty jumpy child. Just about everything and anything scared me. I was picked on a lot by the older ones because I was so skittish. I was gullible and they would laugh about how I would believe everything.

This scared us so bad we started having trouble going into the basement by ourselves. Which some of us never out-grew. We would take someone with us as a lookout guy. We would take turns doing our bathroom business. I felt disgusted that I had to do things this way. I didn't know any other way of handling it at the time. It was our own version of the buddy system. I didn't trust just anyone as my buddy though. I did not know who would want to do what so I was leery who I took with me. As we became adults we didn't know to close the bathroom door. Because of our shared system we didn't know to have privacy.

During the day wasn't much better. At least you could see if there was any blood anywhere. I think most of the time Mother cleaned up the bathroom when things were done. Because I only found blood once more and I was terrified.

There weren't any locks on any of the doors. So if you wanted privacy you had to put a butter knife in the door jam. You had to place the knife so that it was at an angle. Then place the knife between the door and the door frame so that no one could open the door. You just never knew who would walk in on you when you were in the bathroom. It was a pretty scary feeling the not knowing who would be lurking. Not knowing who was peeking in on you while you were in the bathroom was also scary.

I remember many nights waking up in a cold sweat. Waking up dreaming someone was chasing me. Someone was trying to catch me. Someone was just plain trying to get at me. Then I would have trouble going back to sleep because I was afraid I would have these same nightmares all over again.

I didn't know I could pray to God to keep my mind safe. But I know He did keep me safe all the same. During the day when bad things started to happen I would be so afraid I started daydreaming. In this daydream I would see myself floating around on the ceiling watching it from above and not be able to feel a thing. The other place I hid in my mind was a wall at the foot of the stairs. I pretended there was a hidden door there. This place was only for children no adults were allowed. The children were allowed to hide there. It wasn't fun. But you would go there and the pain would be gone. You would be safe and unseen.

I would walk around unseeing and unfeeling so that no one would see me.

The Best Little Double Dutch Jumper

Everyone is good at something. It takes a special person to bring that talent out of their children in such a way that their children want to keep doing it. My mother was that kind of a person. She told me I was the best little double-dutch jumper she had. I loved to jump rope. Our mother and our neighbor would turn the rope. They would take turns allowing their children to jump. Not just the girls either. Mother made sure the boys had a chance to jump. She made sure the girls didn't poke fun at them. This went on every day during the summer. All of us got to be pretty good. We all had a ball. The day that I did the best was really special. I was so proud. Mother said, "Norma you are the best little double-dutch jumper I have." Mother always made sure the others didn't hear it when she said it to one of us. You wouldn't know she told someone else the same thing the day before. Today was the other persons turn to be special.

It wasn't very often that I was singled out for a special compliment. So when mother told me this I just wanted to keep jumping and jumping. I felt special. I couldn't have gotten a better compliment. I tried really hard to do things to perfection. Being the middle kid it was hard to be seen as someone. It was also hard for someone to notice you. When you have so many brothers and sisters everyone is vying for attention. I treasured this memory. As an adult I came to realize she did this to all of her children. We just did not hear her when she told one of the other brothers or sisters how good they were when they did something special. But they told you she said the same thing to them too.

When the neighbor and our mother turned the rope it was the most summer fun we had ever had. I loved summertime with our Mother.

We had little tea parties with our dolls. Mother taught us how to sew. We would make clothes for our dolls. She also taught us to make blankets and pillows for our dolls. This was a time to treasure.

Mother didn't stop there. She also played ball with all of us. She played with the boys and the girls. The older kids were better than the younger ones. Mother had more time with the older children. Mother expected the older ones to teach the younger ones. They didn't though they didn't want the younger kids to be better so they didn't teach us how to throw a ball. They didn't teach us how to play baseball or basketball. The younger boys learned to sew too. They could make clothes for their stuffed animals. It was a really neat way to get new clothes for your doll or teddy bear. We loved to sew new clothes. It was fun. The boys didn't think it was so much fun though. They were called sissies so they quit.

Our mother read her Bible every day. I remember seeing her opening up her Bible and reading. This gave her a peaceful countenance and a glow that could only come from God.

Her special saying was, "Look to God and pray my child that good people can influence your life." I did not understand her relationship with God. It would take a lot of soul searching for me to find this same relationship. I wanted the same relationship my mother had with God. It would take maturity though! Not just in age but in faith.

I didn't realize the importance of this statement until I was older, much older.

96

Mother's Last Christmas

The Christmas of 1958 was one of the best Christmases that I can remember. Christmases were always so special. Mother wanted this one to be extra special. She went to each one of us kids that year and asked us what we wanted for Christmas. She wanted to make sure that we had a special memory. A memory that would last a lifetime that no one could take from us. Some did not know what they wanted. Some of us knew exactly what we wanted. She asked me what I wanted for Christmas. I said, "I want a doll that looks just like me. I wanted a doll with brown hair and brown eyes." Shirley Temple was a popular child movie star. Many little girls craved a Shirley Temple doll for Christmas. Shirley Temple had blonde hair and blue eyes. All my sisters had blonde hair and blue eyes. I looked different. I wanted my doll to look different too. I wanted my doll to look like me instead of my sisters. I loved my sisters but I didn't look much like them.

Mother bought a special present for each one of us kids that year. Do you know how hard it was for her to find a brown haired, brown eyed doll? All the manufacturers were making dolls that looked like Shirley Temple. Very few were making brown haired, brown eyed dolls. Well, it was nearly impossible. But she did find this doll. I took it with me everywhere. She went to bed with me. She ate with me. When I did dishes she was there to watch me. All Karen wanted for Christmas was a watch. Mother got her a watch and she wore it all the time. Vera got a watch too but I don't think she liked it she never wore it. Mother got all the younger girls a doll that looked just like them too. Joan was the youngest girl. She got a doll with a cloth body. The doll was soft and cuddly. Joan's doll had a rubber head with rubber arms and feet. She was a tiny Thumbelina doll. She didn't do anything just made Joan happy. For each one of older boys she bought them a model car. They had to glue the model together. Cars were what they loved best. Model car collections were a big item back then. The youngest boys got metal Tonka trucks and cars.

John and Larry were especially good at gluing these models together. They had been working on cars all of their young lives. They knew without looking at the instructions how and where each part went on these models. They loved model planes too.

It should have been an omen of the things to come. It was almost like she knew it was to be her last Christmas. She must have been in more pain than she let on. No one ever suspected throughout the Christmas Holidays. Everyone was very happy with their presents underneath the tree. Kids think everyone is going to live forever. We didn't know our Mother was sick. The doctors told her two months before Christmas that she was very ill. She needed surgery. But Mother said she wanted to get through the Christmas season first. We didn't know all this though.

The fun and excitement went on all day long. Mother cooked a big dinner with ham, mashed potatoes and gravy. We had Christmas sugar cookies which we got to cut into different shapes to ice. We had some Christmas hard tack ribbon candy too which was my all-time favorite. We helped Mother make candy. Peanut brittle was my next favorite candy we made some of this too. Dad made his specialty old fashioned Hershey's cocoa fudge. Each one of us took a turn stirring it. Dad made the best fudge ever. He knew exactly when the soft ball stage was. He knew exactly when it was ready for stirring and pouring on to a plate. Dad's fudge was always done just right, never too hard or too soft.

Thank you God for giving each of us kids the magic spell of Christmas. Thank you God for letting us see our Dad's good side. Thank you for letting us see his kindnesses during the Christmas season every year. It is a cherished memory. It is a story told over and over again. No one ever gets tired of hearing it. Even our own children and grandchildren can hear these stories. They can see the magic of our shared Christmases. When our children are depressed all we have to do is conjure up the magical Christmas. You can feel the very air vibrate with the enchantment. The story of love shared and love given.

Thank you, God for the memories of the tin train. Thank you God for opening our eyes to letting us see this good. Thank you for letting us see the tin train going around and around the tracks each Christmas. These cherished memories helped us to get through and survive.

We know the true meaning of Christmas. God sent His Son to earth as a baby to save the world from its sin. We know His birthday is celebrated every year at Christmas. But it was also exciting to have the other Christmas celebrations. It made Christmas extra special. It helped us to see a tangible setting instead of just a feeling.

Mother didn't have any time to waste. She was too busy seeing to everyone else's needs. She wasn't taking care of herself. She had sewn together some doll clothes like she always did. She wrapped them all herself. She tied all the packages with pretty little ribbons and bows for the girls. All the other Christmases paled in comparison to this one. It might have been because God (Jesus) was right there in the midst of us. He was waiting to take our Mother home with Him. She was tired and worn out. Jesus knows all the right things to say and do to bring us comfort. He was bringing Mother comfort this Christmas and we were reaping all the benefits from it. We did not know she was sick.

Mother couldn't have been happier. She was making her family happy. This is just what she wanted to do. She wanted to give her family one last memory of her at Christmas time. I loved my doll. It looked just like me we were inseparable. It had brown eyes and brown curly hair. She had a painted on smile. Her eyes didn't close. But they were brown she was special to me. Mother made this the best Christmas ever.

The tin train went around and around the Christmas tree and the Christmas village. We were very happy and the train didn't pick up any passengers this year either. We watched as the smoke stack blew. The whistle blew. The light came on the little tin train. We would take the horns down from the tree and blow them. The little toy soldiers would be taken down and they would march. We had to help them but their arms and legs moved.

Dad made sure all the ornaments on the tree were real with real moving parts.

Mother's Illness

     Right after the Christmas Holidays Mother had some more tests run. It did not take the hospital long to call mother back with the test results. The nurse said, "We have a room ready for you Mrs. Baas. It is imperative that you come into the hospital to have the surgery. Mrs. Baas you can no longer afford to put this surgery off." I remember seeing the phone fall out of my Mother's hands they were shaking out of control. I remember seeing my Mother almost fall over while leaning on the wall until my Dad grabbed her. I remember mother and dad hugging each other. Mother was crying so hard, that dad started to cry also. I didn't understand it all then. But I too felt the pain they were suffering. I did not know at the time that this would be one of the last phone calls mother ever got from the hospital. She had surgery shortly after the New Year had begun.

Mother went into the hospital. The cancer that was spotted during the delivery of Daryl had spread rapidly. It was all over her intestinal tract. The doctors did a complete hysterectomy. They removed some of her large intestines and small intestines.

She was in the hospital for several days. She came home with a colostomy bag on her side for her small and large intestinal. I did not know what it was but it looked ominous. It was seeping something I couldn't tell what. Dad wouldn't let anyone else touch our mother. He was the only person who was allowed clean her up.

Both of my parents wanted to keep it a secret as to how bad she really was. They kept praying for a miracle. The doctors too were hoping for a miracle. The

106

doctors knew the circumstances at home and how many young children she had. They were keeping their hopes up that she would get better. So in order to do this no one could touch my mother. My mother's sister tried to help once and dad said, "leave her alone I will do it myself."

Dad stayed sober during mother's illness. He made all kinds of promises to our mother about staying sober. She just needed to get better so that he could keep these promises. Dad was up around the clock catering to all mother's needs. My mother's sister (Aunt Ann) had five kids of her own. When Auntie Ann could break away from her duties like house cleaning and caring for her own children in Spring-field, Ohio she drove in just to see her sister.

Dad and mother had cooked up the scheme of not letting on how seriously ill our mother was. They wanted to keep everyone from worrying. They wanted to keep us kids from getting upset about the possibility of her dying. They wanted to keep the sympathy and questions at bay. It was our parents wishes that no one know.

What my parents failed to realize was that mother's loved ones should have a chance to prepare for the outcome of the situation. It's far easier on the people left behind if they can prepare themselves mentally for the outcome no matter what that may be. They think children don't understand but they do. As anyone who experienced this at a young age my advice would be to tell them every detail of the situation no matter how precarious it is. Children do understand. They see death all the time in Gods creations. They see it when butterflies die. They see it when their beloved pets die. They see it in the passing of the seasons when the grasses are all dried up from the heat of summer and in the winter when the leaves on the trees have died.

Mother and Dad tried to push it away how bad off she really was. They did not want to think about it. Maybe they thought it was best for us. Maybe they were hoping and praying for a different outcome. Maybe they wanted to keep their own spirits up. We will never know.

Mother made Dad promise to give up drinking and he did give it up. Dad was with Mother around the clock. He would not allow anyone else to tend to her needs. He didn't really do much work at his garage that whole time. Dad didn't really work while our mother was sick. Jr. our oldest brother took over the managing of the affairs of the garage business. He was sixteen years old. A very hefty job for one so young! He had been helping Dad out ever since before he went to school. Jr. knew the operations of the garage. He knew how to distribute the work. Dad had been drunk all the time anyway. Most of the time, Dad was passed out drunk either on the floor or in one of the many cars that were around.

Mother made Dad promise to keep us in Sunday school too.

I was not prepared the first time I saw the changing of the colostomy bag. It smelled so bad it stunk up the whole living room. I was disgusted. Dad saw me and told me to get out. He didn't want me to come back in. I did leave but not before I smelled the rank odor. I was shocked. I didn't know things like this existed. I wasn't prepared. My Mother and I had been inseparable. I was clingy to my Mother. I had done a lot for her. I tried to help her out as much as possible. I tried to lighten her load. Now Dad was always there so I could no longer help her. I shouldn't have been hurt. I was always the one Mother depended upon to help her out. Now she depended on Dad. I wasn't needed anymore.

Mother was really tired at first for the first few weeks. She slept most of the time. This was almost impossible with so many kids around. Then she rallied a little. She was able to start taking in some food. Not much food just enough to rally her. I think she was still in the mode of protecting her children. So she forced herself to keep going. She started to get some color back into her skin.

Dad fed our Mother. Dad bathed her. He literally wouldn't let anyone come near her. None of us kids dared to make a noise while she was sleeping. Dad would be so mad you would wish you hadn't riled him up. When you saw Dad taking care of our Mother like he was, it made you forget the ugliness that transpired before. With as much abuse as we had already suffered it was hard to forgive and forget when that is all you knew. It was hard to do what the Bible said to do like honor your Father and Mother when you are an abused child. A child becomes confused as to what is right and what is wrong?

I loved my Mother and didn't want to see her suffering. I didn't know how to help her. I would have helped if they had told me to help. I felt like I was no longer needed. I felt like I was losing control. If I would have been told what to expect perhaps I may have felt differently.

Dad's Garage

By the time Mother was ill Dad had raised three strong sons to take over the garage (mechanic) business. He let them run the garage while he tended to Mother's needs. Jr. was sixteen by this time. Jr. was the oldest boy. He was now in charge. He was five foot six inches tall. He had blue eyes. He had dark blonde hair. His hair was very curly and very unruly. In order to tame his hair he had to add some hair cream to his hair. He took his job of caring for the family business seriously. He never got paid. He just did what was expected. Everyone respected him. The customers, the parts dealers respected and trusted Jr. They knew Jr. knew what he was doing. Everyone liked Jr. He was very friendly and knowledgeable. He had a memory like an elephant. He never forgot a name. He never forgot a face. He could tell you and describe every detail of an engine or a transmission. Plus he could tell you what each part could do. Jr. could take apart the whole car and put it back together. All he had to do was read a book and it was there in his memory banks forever.

Larry was nine years old. He was the quiet one. He did what he was told. He never caused trouble unless John was around. He had dark hair too not dark brown but dark blond. He had blue eyes which depending upon his mood would turn hazel. He also knew every angle and every aspect of the car. He could see a part and know exactly which car it was from. In those days each car was distinct from the others. They could see a bumper and know which car it came from.

114

John was eight years old. He was ornery. Anytime he could get out of working and sneak away he did. Usually John would drag Larry right along with him. Then Larry would get into trouble. John would say well Larry made me do it. Cause Dad wouldn't whip Larry. But he sure would take a belt to John. He was trouble with a capital T. But John knew cars as much as his two older brothers his passion for the cars was custom building though. But his first passion was for speed. He wanted to be a race car driver but dad wouldn't let him do it. He did race though the illegal kind. He usually won too. He loved fast cars.

They weren't exactly adults. But the business had to be kept afloat or there wouldn't be any food on the table. There wouldn't be any money to pay the doctor bills that seemed to be mounting. Since Dad was home most days now. He was a lot quieter. He wasn't his usual loud mouth uncouth self. He always acted this way after he had been drinking.

The Boys went to school. Then they went straight to the garage. All this before they were even allowed to come home and eat supper. After they ate they had to be bathed and put to bed. John and Larry were too tired to wake up enough to get washed up for bed. A lot of the time it was three o'clock in the morning before they came home. By six o'clock they were up again just to start all over.

In the morning the girls had to wake the boys up to get them ready for school. It was not an easy task waking the boys up after they had been up working so late. Three or four hours sleep just didn't seem like a reasonable amount of time to keep them going.

Dad may have been home tending to our Mother. But he knew exactly what jobs were at the garage. Who they belonged to! So if the boys were not producing like Dad thought they should. They would get hit with the belt Dad was always wearing. He would use it without any hesitation. When Dad said jump you asked, "How high?" In today's society we call this micro managing. The customers would call Dad up on the phone too. If they didn't like something that was being done then the boys got into real trouble. He would yell at the boys for this too.

My Dad was no little man. He was a lot bigger than the boys. So when he took his belt off you knew what was going to happen next. The boys learned to toe the line. When Dad said something or asked you to do something you did it immediately. You did not question his methods. Dad was not afraid to use methods that would be considered abuse in today's society.

The boys never had the gentle hand of our mother to raise them. Only our Dad at the garage was the only discipline they knew. All the riffraff that hung around down there at the garage were not a good influence either. It was not a pleasant atmosphere in which to raise boys. Mother made Dad promise to get the boys home early. She wanted them to finish their education. He promised her that he'd not make them work so hard. He started letting them come home before midnight. So during Mother's illness the boys got to come home before midnight.

Because of his mother's influence, my Dad was not the type to kowtow to a woman. So whenever possible he made the boys work harder and longer. He often said that: "No boy of mine is going to be hanging onto his mother's skirt strings." He wanted to make all the boys go to the garage. Mother wouldn't hear of it. John was the last of the boys who went to the garage. Mother would not budge on this.

Dad gets Hepatitis

Dad came down with hepatitis a few weeks into mother's illness. Mother had already had her surgery. Dad had been the only one who was taking care of her. Mother was beside herself with worry. She not only had to worry about her husband but also about her children getting hepatitis. She had a lot of young children. She was too sick to take care of them by herself. So Grandma Lamb came in to help again. Hepatitis is a highly contagious disease. Dad was hospitalized for a few days. They removed Dad form the situation. None of the doctors knew how he had contacted this disease. Mother's doctors were afraid she would also get hepatitis. Her immune system was so low. They were afraid of the complications this would cause her.

Unfortunately, Dad wasn't the only one who came down with hepatitis. My oldest brother Jr. and my oldest sister Vera also came down with it. Jr. was in the hospital several days. The garage business was in jeopardy. Vera was in the hospital for several weeks. Vera hated dad for giving her this disease. Dad did do a lot of drinking. When he was drunk he drank whatever was in a glass. He didn't even care whose glass it was. If there was liquid in the glass he drank from it. So maybe this is what caused the hepatitis. We will never know and the doctors never told us. Maybe it was from caring for mother all these weeks.

When the doctors heard there were nine other children in our household and the rest of us could possibly have this disease they ordered us all to get a shot. We all got a hepatitis shot to keep us well. They wanted to keep us from infecting other kids. We could have given it to the kids at school. This may have caused an epidemic. They wanted to keep us from infecting our mother too. I remember how the shot hurt and burned. It went away after a few days. It felt like someone had burnt my arm where the needle point had been. The nurse wasn't very nice about it either. She grabbed and yanked my arm and stuck the needle in. She thought we were dirty people. She thought this was how we had contacted the disease. The nurse said as much. That hurt too. I suppose that when you are dealing with this many children the first thing you think of is how dirty these people are. Not whether they have feelings. Just something or someone caused these trashy people to get hepatitis. It wasn't caused by cleanliness.

We were not taught boundaries in our house. We were all just lumped together as a unit from the oldest to the youngest. Numerical order so to speak. When people came to visit it was easier to have us line up from the oldest to the youngest to tell us apart. No names were used. They would say things like, "Which number are you." I would say, "Number Six."

If we wanted a drink and it belonged to someone else we took a drink. If we needed a hair brush we used the first one that we ran across. We didn't care. No one told us not to share these types of things. It wasn't too often we brushed our own hair. Mother always did this for us. We didn't know that germs were passed on this way. By sharing things like glasses of water or cool-aide we passed on germs. So this is probably how the germs were passed around to each other.

We were not taught any kind of cleanliness habits either. As far as tooth brushes are concerned we didn't own any. They were not a concern to my parents. To have your own tooth brush was unheard of. There was one small bathroom. Our small bathroom didn't have any counter top space. There wasn't any place to put things like tooth brushes. We didn't have tooth paste either. No one ever taught us not to share things like tooth brushes. No one ever put tooth brush holders on the wall. We shared everything! We even shared our germs because we were not taught any better. So the doctors were right in getting us the shot. It very well could possibly have been an epidemic with all of us kids spreading the germs at school.

We didn't own dressers either. All of our clothes were put into boxes, bags and baskets. So needless to say all of our clothes were crammed into these boxes and bags and baskets. They were stacked one on top of the other. Our clothes looked dirty and wrinkled before we even put our clothes on. Can you imagine a two bed-room house with eleven dressers? Our bedrooms weren't that big either. There just wasn't any more room for that many dressers. So the boxes, bags and baskets of clothes were everywhere there was a spare corner. Everywhere the eye could see there was a bag of clothes or a box of clothes or a basket of clothes. We tried to keep them in the bedrooms to keep the house some-what organized. It was hard to tell what bag or box or basket belonged to whom. They were not labeled either. We had an old ringer washer and we hung the clothes up on a clothes line. These old ringer washers were a long, drawn-out process. We didn't own a dryer either. Electric or gas to run the dryer would have cost too much money. The dryer too would have been expensive. It took a long time to wash the clothes at our house. Hanging the clothes on the clothesline in the basement or outside took another day or two, depending upon the weather. Luckily we didn't own too many outfits. Nothing like today's kids own, three or four outfits a day goes into the wash.

We shared the bath water too. No one wanted to be the last person or the last kid to take a bath. When the eleventh child got into the water it was pretty dirty. I hated taking a bath after everyone else. I didn't feel like I was getting clean. Most of the time, the older kids pushed the younger kids out of the way to be first. This is when the oldest to the youngest was strictly enforced. I was kid number six and there was still five after me. We the younger kids hated always being last. To this day we still hate being last, we laugh about it now, sometimes.

Luckily we didn't take a bath every day. However this created a whole new set of problems. We looked dirty. We smelled dirty. We were called white trash by our friends. They probably got the name from their parents. The neighbors in the neighborhood called us white trash too. Everyone avoided us like the plague. I think they were afraid it was going to rub off onto them or their children. It was another one of those times I felt shame. It made me feel like my family was vastly different from other people. I felt that others looked down on us. I knew we were different but it wasn't until I became an adult that I knew exactly how different we really were.

None of the rest of us got hepatitis. My mother was starting to get around a little. She was starting to take care of herself. She still couldn't keep up with eleven children and the house cleaning or the cooking. Grandma Lamb helped out a lot.

My mother's sister from Springfield came into Columbus a lot to help. Dad couldn't throw her out now.

Mother Gets Her Driver's License

In February of 1959 my mother got her driver's license. Dad had finally taught her how to drive. She was so happy. She was ecstatic over it as a matter of fact. After she came home from getting her driver's license she piled all of us kids into the station wagon. Dad had just bought for her. She took us for a ride around the block. We were so happy for her so excited. After all those weeks of her recuperation from her surgery it was good to have something to celebrate. It was hard not to contain your excitement when someone else is so excited. It was not a common thing for a woman to drive back then. Mother loved every minute of it. We all loved sharing it with her. She was so proud. She had finally done something she had wanted to do for a long-time. Mother wanted to drive a car. Grandma Lamb her mother drove a car. Grandma Lamb was a lot older than our mother. She wanted to not be so dependent upon everyone else. For once in her life she wanted her independence. If the kids were sick she wanted to be the one who took them to the doctor. At the end of February she turned thirty-five. I think she also wanted to show us girls to not be so dependent. She wanted us to be independent.

It wasn't easy for our mother to do these things either. She still had to wear the colostomy bag. She still had to maintain the sterile environment of keeping this area clean. She had to make sure it was emptied and not leaking. It would get heavy. It was in the way. She was able to hide it under the baggie house dresses she always wore. She had to wear it with her everywhere she went. If not than all this fluid would back up into her body. This fluid would have killed her. She even had it on when she went for her driver's license. She could not take the chance of getting an infection.

It was like Mother was in a mad dash to get things done. She wanted to do things she had kept putting off. It was hard to do some things when you have so many kids to keep an eye on. I think Mother knew her time on this earth was limited. This is why she was in such a mad dash to get things done. She wanted to do things she hadn't done before. See things she hadn't seen before.

Mother was so proud of getting her driver's license. She started driving herself to the store. She drove herself down to our dad's garage. She wanted to show off her newly acquired skills. She drove the car to her mother's house. She drove to Spring-field where her sister lived. Daryl had been at Auntie Anne's house practically since he was born. Mother had been too sick to nurse him. Auntie Anne was still breast feeding her youngest one. So she took on the responsibility of our youngest brother too. Mother needed to see for herself that Daryl was ok. Daryl had a really severe case of pneumonia as well. This worried Mother. She brought him back home with her where he belonged.

Mother and Dad were doing their best keeping her illness a secret. Not telling anyone how seriously ill she really was. They didn't want to worry any of us kids. They didn't want to worry mother's mother Grandma Lamb with how bad she was. Grandma knew though she was a nurse's aide. But if one looked close enough you could see that she wasn't getting any better. She didn't have the luxury of another day. So each new day became more precious than the day before.

She drove everywhere she could until she was just too worn out to go out anymore. But the excitement lingered on. She had gotten to the point in her illness where she was tired of laying around. No rest and no peace here though not with eleven kids all running around all the time. All of us kids played as normal. We went to school as normal. We were oblivious to the undercurrents that were going on in our house. We were going on as business as usual. But this is what she wanted. She wanted us around her for as long as she could have us with her. She wanted us to remember her. The only way for this to happen was for us to spend time with her. That is exactly what happened.

It was like Mother had her list of things she still wanted to accomplish. She just started doing them. Today we would call it a bucket list. She was not going to waste precious time. The more she did the more she wanted to do.

She was not going to take this illness lying down. She fought to stay alert for the sake of her children. It was a testament of her love for us. She still got us off to church on Sundays. She got us off to school the rest of the week. Even though she didn't feel up to going to church she made sure we always went. She made our dad promise to continue to do the same thing too. We didn't understand it at the time. Why was she in such a hurry to do things she had been putting off? It was like she didn't have much time left and she knew it. She wanted to accomplish as much as she could in a short span of time. She must have realized there wasn't too much time left for her. I have heard it said when you are dying you know it. I think she knew it.

When springtime came this year mother would still go outside on those beautiful sunny mornings. She would rock and swing the youngest of the children on the porch swing. She would sing lullabies to them. I think she was hoping they too would remember her. Joan and Jimmy the twins remember her. They remember a dark haired woman swinging them. They remember her rocking them to sleep. They turned three the day after our mother died. Jim and Joan didn't look much like twins. Jimmy has dark hair almost black like our mother's. He also had brown eyes like our mother too. Joan had dishwater blond hair like our dad's. She also had the prettiest pale blue eyes like our dad too. Jimmy was also twice the size of Joan. Jimmy was born 5 minutes before Joan so he was the oldest. Joan and Jimmy both were happy all the time. When they smiled, they lit up the whole room.

Easter came and went this year without too much of a mishap. Daryl was home with our Mother she wanted to keep her children with her. We all went to Grandma Baas's house for Easter. She cooked a huge dinner for all of her children and grandchildren. All my dad's brothers and sisters and their children were there. Mother is not in any of the pictures so she must not have gone to Grandma's house.

For Easter this year Grandma Baas bought all the boys a suit or dress pants and a shirt and tie. I think she knew that mother's time on this earth was shortened too. She probably knew the boys would be needing suits if there was a funeral. Not to be out done either Grandma Lamb bought all the girls an Easter dress and a bonnet. I had never had a store bought dress before. I had always gotten Karen's or Vera's hand me downs. I was so proud of that dress. We didn't know they had an ulterior motive for buying them. We looked sharp. We even got new shoes and socks. It was a rarity for us to get new shoes. We always got socks but this year we got both. We always got hand me down shoes too. No one ever thought that by the time the older brothers and sisters were done wearing them they might be worn out.

136

Uncle John Comes for a Visit

Shortly after Easter in May of 1959 our mother went back to the Dr.'s office. The Dr. told our mother they had not gotten all of her cancer. It had spread so rapidly there wasn't anything more they could do for her. She had waited too long for her original surgery. They had done their best but he could see there wasn't much time left. They told her she had at the most six months. He told my mother she needed to get her affairs in order. Mother was in and out of the hospital during the last few weeks she was alive.

They did finally tell all the family members except their kids. They still kept it from all of us. Mother spent her last few days in the hospital. She did not want us kids to see her die. She wanted us to remember her as she was. She did not want us to remember her dying. Wasting away with all the infections she was getting.

The hospital called all the relatives and told them that if they wanted to say their good-byes to our Mother they needed to get to the hospital right away. By this time mother had taken a turn for the worse. Mother and dad were still praying and hoping for a better outcome. But they didn't tell us kids.

My mother's brother John flew in from the state of Washington to say his good-byes. He took the first flight out that he could get.

As Uncle John came walking through the door, all of us kids including my cousins were scared. The cousins were spending the nights with us, Aunt Anne's children. This saved her from having to drive back and forth every day from Springfield. We took off up the stairs. We were terrified of this strange man. He just came walking in without knocking like he knew what he was doing. But as soon as he saw some of us peeking around the corner he said, "Hi, I'm Uncle John." We were all whispering amongst ourselves, "Uncle John." Heck we had all heard stories of Uncle John. We felt like we knew Uncle John. We were still afraid and apprehensive. We had never met him before. It didn't take him long to surmise the situation he said, "Anyone want some ice-cream and seven-up." We all hollered in unison, "Pop and ice-cream." He knew how to win the hearts of the coldest child. What kid wouldn't want ice-cream and pop? For most families it was a rare treat to get ice-cream. But for large families it was rarer still a real novelty. We ran down the stairs as fast as our legs would carry us. We were yelling the whole time, "I do, I do" in unison. We were afraid now if we didn't hurry it would all be gone before we got any. We ran into the kitchen and Uncle John was already dipping and filling the bowls with ice-cream. He knew he had altered our dreary existence even if only for a moment. He loved his sister. It showed in how he took charge of helping us out even for a moment. He was and still is a wonderful man.

Uncle John became the family's favorite uncle. From that day forward we all sang his praises. He had a kind word and a hug for each one of us kids. He knew what we had been through with our dad. Not once did he ever try to undermine our mother's and dad's authority. He did not try to down grade my dad to any of us kids. Nor did he treat us with anything but respect. He treated us as equals. He did not treat us as children. We learned to love him for it. We never forgot it. It is just too bad he lived so far away. He may have been able to help but then he may have brought tragedy upon his own family. He had a wife and two children of his own to care for. Some of his wife's family lived in the state of Washington. This is where he settled with his family.

Uncle John did make it to the hospital just in time to see his sister one last time.

Grandma Lamb was with our mother when she died. Mother died on Memorial Day, May 30th, 1959. That was the day they used to celebrate Memorial Day. Mother was worried about us kids and what would become of us. She kept asking her mother saying, "What will happen to my children? Who will take care of my children?" Finally Grandma Lamb said, "God will take care of your children Ella. Don't you worry? He will take care of everything for you. They are safe in His loving and capable arms." After Grandma said this, Mother died peacefully in her arms saying, "Oh Mother it is so beautiful here, so beautiful. I see Him Mother." She died with the most beautiful smile on her face as she breathed her last breath.

The nurses promised my Mother that they would bring ice-cream and cake for the twin's birthday. The twin's birthday is on May 31 but she never made it to see their third birthday.

Uncle John left shortly after the funeral to go home. He went back to the state of Washington. He never liked how our Dad treated his sister. Now that she was gone there wasn't any need to stay.

Mother's Funeral

I am standing here in this strange place I have never seen before. As an adult I realize it must have been the funeral parlor. Strangers brought me here. I can't even tell you where I have been. I didn't know the people. I kept crying I wanted to go home. They wouldn't let me go home. I haven't seen my brothers and sisters for a few days. I haven't seen my Mother either for a few days. I look around at all these people dressed in black. No one I know was even here. I started wondering off looking around for someone I knew.

I was scared. There wasn't anyone I knew. All of a sudden I see her, my Mother. She is in this strange bed I have never seen before sleeping, or so I thought. So I touched her and said, "Mother wake up! Mother wake up please! I'm scared. I don't know what to do. Please help me Mother." I started screaming hysterically at the top of my lungs. My Mother was hard and cold. I try shaking her to make her wake up. She doesn't even budge. She just lies there cold and hard without any life to her.

Grandma Baas comes over immediately along with a few other people I don't know. They start shaking me and shaking me. This makes me feel worse. They tell me to shut up this instant I was making a scene. I didn't even know what a scene was let alone know that I was making one. Someone says, "Norma you shut up this instant." I didn't. I didn't know how to quit screaming. So I was smacked into submission except that didn't make me stop screaming either. It made me scream all the harder.

I said, "I want my Mother. I want her to wake up." They told me she is not here. I said, "Oh yes she is, she is right over there," and I pointed to where she was. "I tried to make her wake up but she just won't wake up." Grandma Baas said, "Get this brat out of here. Get her out of here now! Whatever you do don't let the other younger ones come in here. She is the oldest of the younger ones. If she is this hysterical imagine how the others are going to be." So they took me out of this building still screaming at the top of my lungs. I am kicking and screaming the whole way. It was not like me to throw such a fit. I just wanted my mother and no one would help me see her. No one would help me wake her up.

I am six years old. Two weeks shy of my seventh birthday.

All my younger brothers and sisters never got to see our Mother again. There are five of them Debbie five and a half, Freddie four and a half, the twins (Jimmy and Joan) had just turned three, and Daryl was ten months old. I didn't see any of them. They never got to see our Mother ever again. I didn't see any of my older brothers and sisters either. I must have been the first to arrive.

No one once tried to console me. No one once tried to tell me it was ok to cry. No one once held me to tell me Mother had died. She was in heaven with Jesus. Just smack, smack to make me quit screaming. It didn't make me quit though. It just made me scream all the more. It just made me more hysterical.

So the people who had brought me here took me back to their place. I kept crying, "I want my Mother. Why was she so cold? Why was she in that place?" No answer here either. They stopped at the store. I sat in the car along with the woman whom I didn't know. My screaming had finally subsided a little. I am crying and hiccupping both at the same time. They didn't want to take me into the store acting the way I was. So I stayed in the car crying. I think they were afraid to leave me alone for fear I would run away. So they did not leave me alone.

This man had dark hair and dark brown eyes. I could have passed for his daughter. His wife did all the talking. Probably a good thing since my dad made me not trust men. The lady had dark hair and brown eyes a round face so I could have passed for her daughter as well. I just didn't want to be their daughter. I wanted to go home.

Later as an adult I learned that the lady was Aunt Ruth. She was one of my mother's aunts. They could have gotten to know me when my mother was alive. Instead of trying to force the issue after my mother was dead. It would have made it easier for adjustment. They could have acted as if they cared instead of trying to pretend that my feelings mattered.

The man is finally done shopping. So we drove back to their place. They tell me they have always wanted a little girl. They never had children of their own. They asked me if I would like to be their child. All I said, "I want my Mother. I have a Mother. I want my brothers and sisters. I want to go home." They pretended they did not to hear me. The man said,

"I bought you some cold cereal and some ice-cream. I also bought you some pop." They both said "What kind of cereal do you like?" Again they said, "We bought several different kinds of cereal. What kind do you like?" Still I didn't answer them. I just kept crying, "I want to go home." "I want my Mother and my brothers and sisters, I want to go home. I want my Mother to wake up." They never once tried to tell me my Mother was dead and that she was never coming home again. They put me to bed thinking that this might console me. It seems I have been here a long time.

To a kid whose mother has just left them they feel abandoned. I do not know how long I have been here but a kid does not really understand the concept of time. They feel somehow at fault for not being loving enough. They feel they should have done something differently. They blame themselves for all the tragedies that are going on. Not being allowed to go home upset me a lot. I wanted to see everyone at home.

Finally, this couple took me home. Not once during this two week period was I ever told that my Mother had died. Not once did anyone tell me she wasn't ever coming back. I was inconsolable. I cried all the time. I would not talk to anyone either. No one would have listened anyway. These people were trying to get me to like them but they were not being successful. They were going about it all wrong.

150

The Big Family Meeting

Finally after two weeks this couple brought me back home. I am the first to arrive. I run through the house looking for someone I knew. I said, "Hi! Is anyone here? I am back. I have missed you guys." I ran around and around none of my brothers and sisters are here. No one is here. I am all alone. I am crying hysterically again. Did all my brothers and sisters go away too? I heard this couple tell whoever was in charge that I was inconsolable. All that I wanted to do was cry. They said, "All she wanted was to go home. She wanted to see her brothers and sisters so we brought her back. We don't know what to do with a child like her."

Grandma and Grandpa Baas finally arrive. They were not happy with the results of finding me back home either. No one else did though. Slowly after what seemed like hours everyone else starts arriving. Slowly ever so slowly they are trickling in to our house. All the Aunts and Uncles started arriving. All of my brothers and sisters started arriving too because they have been with the aunts and uncles. Karen, Daryl, and Vera had been at Auntie Anne's in Springfield. The twins were with Aunt Claire and Uncle Bob. The boys (Jr. Larry and John) and Dad had gone to Grandma and Grandpa Baas's house to stay. Where Dad went the older boys would go. They were mostly at the garage with Dad. Debbie and Freddie were with strangers they didn't know either. Pretty scary! Debbie said she was locked away in a dark room a lot. She couldn't remember very much of anything else. Debbie said, "The room was a small closet, small and tiny. She said it did not have any windows. The room seemed airless." She did say they took them out separately. But she can't remember what they did when they were allowed out of this room. I still don't understand why they would give us to people we did not know?

Grandma and Grandpa Baas mostly Grandma have decided that they would hold a big family meeting. But Grandpa didn't stop Grandma either. They wanted to figure out what to do with us kids. It is a really big family meeting they are having. That is why everyone is congregating at our house. They did not know what to do with all of us, the children. Grandma Baas said, "There is an orphanage in Michigan."

One of the most important people who should be involved isn't. My Dad had no idea that a big family meeting was about to go on and he was not invited. He had gone back to work to put food on the table. He had no idea anything like this was going on behind his back. This was all his mother's doing. My dad is 44 years old and his mother is still running his life for him. Should I say ruining his life? He wasn't even invited. Dad's best friend the guy who owned the building he rented for the garage business called and asked Dad why he wasn't invited to the big family meeting. My Dad said, "What family meeting?" This guy said, "The one your Mother called together." My dad said, "What the hell are you talking about." This guy said, "Oh you really don't know do you?"

Dad said, "Does this sound like a guy who knows about a family meeting?" The guy said, "Well no! Now that you mention it, it doesn't sound like you knew." So this guy said, "Your mother called a family meeting together. They are deciding what to do about your children." Dad said, "What do you mean? What to do about my children. Where is it any of their business? By God will they never quit meddling into things that do not concern them?" My dad's best friend knew how my Grandma Baas was. He also knew it didn't matter how old my dad was his mother would never quit interfering into her son's life.

Dad came home and he was furious. He could not believe his family was doing this to him. He said, "No one will take my kids away from me." His Mother said, "Who will watch them while you work." Dad said, "That will be none of your business. You never liked Ella from the beginning. You will not take her children from this house. Get out of my house now before I throw you out! Do not come back." Grandma Baas started to say something else but Grandpa finally spoke up and said, "Frieda! Stay out of it. This doesn't concern you. Let Art raise his own children. Let's go home. We don't belong here." Grandma Baas said, "But who will help him." Grandpa said, "That is not our concern." Grandma Lamb finally spoke up and said, "I will help Art with the children. They are my grandchildren too."

Today is my birthday.

I turned 7 years old today.

No one remembered.

Epilogue

These stories are true to the best of my abilities. These things and more happened to each and every one of us kids. This is just a small sampling of some of what we had to endure. While our mother was still alive more could have been added.

These stories here contain only the first seven years of my life and the lives of my brothers and sisters. As I got older the abuse was often worse. That is why I am writing it all down. I am hoping to stop the abuse for some poor child. Even if I stop the abuse of just one child it will have been worth it. Reliving the pain and suffering all over again.

I am also hoping to solve some of the family's mysteries for the future generations. I do not want them to make some of the same mistakes we made. When we were raising our children the abuse must stop.

I have four more books in The Tin Train series. I have the years we lived with our Grandma Lamb. I also have the years we lived with our step-mother. I also have the years we were finally put into an orphanage. Then of course my dad's garage, which is the final book in The Tin Train Series of my childhood memories.

As I age the stories of abuse that I hear and feel seem to get worse.

If you are a parent and see yourself in any of these situations, please seek help to stop the abuse. Do not allow your anger to get the best of your child.

If you are a child and are being abused please seek help from a trusted friend. You don't have to go through it alone. You are not alone.

My advice to new parents is this if you loved what your parents did for you then do these things for your child. If your parents did things that you hated, then do not do these things to your child. If by chance you were a child who suffered similar situations than beware to be careful not to do to your child these things. Only you with the help of God and our Lord and Savior Jesus Christ can you stop the abuse.

Bring about normal healthy productive citizens.

Your children just want you to love them.

Watch for the next book of the Tin Train Series,

"The North Wind"

Grandma Comes to Stay.

Made in the USA
Charleston, SC
25 March 2013